Autobiography of Jumbo's Keeper,

and

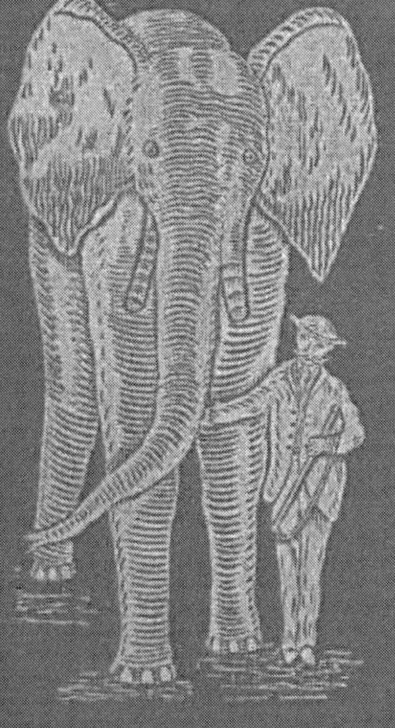

Jumbo's Biography

SECTION OF SHIP
Showing position
of JUMBO
ENGINE

AUTOBIOGRAPHY

OF

MATTHEW SCOTT

JUMBO'S KEEPER

FORMERLY OF THE ZOÖLOGICAL SOCIETY'S GARDENS,
LONDON, AND RECEIVER OF SIR EDWIN
LANDSEER MEDAL IN 1866

ALSO

JUMBO'S BIOGRAPHY

BY THE SAME AUTHOR

BRIDGEPORT, CONN.
TROW'S PRINTING AND BOOKBINDING CO., NEW YORK
1885

Jumbo's Keeper: The autobiography of Matthew Scott and his biography of P.T. Barnum's great elephant Jumbo

ISBN-13: 978-1480107984
ISBN-10: 1480107980

facebook.com/bamberbooks

DEDICATION.

I TAKE great pleasure in dedicating this book, containing my autobiography and the biography of Jumbo, to the people of the United States of America and Great Britain.

I have travelled through the United States, North, East, South, and West, and have received in my travels the greatest kindness. If "Jumbo" could but speak, I know he would endorse what I say here. I have had the same experience in Great Britain, and the spirit of gratitude impels me to acknowledge my appreciation of the good will of the people of both countries, by dedicating my humble efforts to them, hoping that this attempt may be received with the same kindness that has been always extended to me in person.

Respectfully,

MATTHEW SCOTT.

BRIDGEPORT, CONN.,
January 14, 1885.

MY AUTOBIOGRAPHY.

CHAPTER I.

MY BIRTH-PLACE AND START IN LIFE.

I purpose giving to the world, for the benefit of my fellow-men, my humble and truthful history. I have many times thought I would do so, not for my own glory, but for the enlightenment of such people as are anxious to obtain knowledge. It is only to-day, January 14, 1885, that I have concluded to set about writing it, and I purpose to give a faithful record of my life, setting forth the various experiences through which I have passed.

I was born at Knowsley, Lancashire, England, in 1834. It was the seat of Lord

Derby, the grandfather of the present earl; and from a child I learned to love that family.

The Earls of Derby were, and are, among the greatest statesmen of England.

My start in life was very humble, and I have even now, in my fifty-first year, very little to boast of with regard to this world's goods. I have lived with Jumbo day and night for twenty years of my life. I am what is called a "self-made man," and can boast that the knowledge and experience I possess, I have learned while living with wild beasts, latterly in the company of my friend and companion "Jumbo," the greatest known animal on earth. I suppose my companion and I have seen more human faces than most people, and I have spoken to as many people as almost any other man. My life has been, perhaps, as peculiar and checkered as that of any man of my time of life; yet I claim nothing but to show to the people of the United States and Great Britain, to whom this book is dedicated, what an humble son of toil has passed through in the precarious, though to me, pleasant, occupation of keeper, breeder, and lover of the beasts and birds of the forests and fields of all countries and climes.

CHAPTER II.

MY FIRST EXPERIENCE AS A KEEPER.

I have already remarked in the previous chapter that I was born at Knowsley, near Liverpool, England, on the estate of Lord Derby. My father was born at the same place, and was "brewer" to the earl.

My dear, good, and much-loved mother was born on the same estate.

Our family consisted of sixteen sons and one daughter—a goodly number—and I am the fifteenth son (though "better late than never").

I lost my dear father when I was four years old—he lived to the age of three score years and ten.

My mother lived to survive him several years.

When I was sent to London in 1851, I left the dear old soul hearty and in good spirits, proud of her boy's going up to the biggest city in the world. I verily believe the good woman thought her fifteenth son was going to turn out something unusual. Although she used to say that I was "a rough, naughty lad, full of devilment," she also said, in her quaint way, "if you take that lad and strip him naked, and put him on top of a mountain anywhere on the globe, he can get his own living; for, if there's nobody round the neighborhood of the mountain, he will have the birds and animals feed him, like old Elijah and the raven in the wilderness, or, like John the Baptist, he will live on locusts and honey, and clothe himself with the skins of animals."

Oh! my dear young readers, such a mother is worth more to you than all the world. You just listen to your mother, and mark every word she says when she advises and directs you, and you cannot fail to get along in life.

I returned from London to Knowsley to visit the dear soul once before she died.

However, to continue my story, I grew up at Knowsley, and at ten years of age was engaged to feed the feathered tribes at the private menagerie of the earl, who was a great lover of birds and beasts, and who spent much time and money in their importation and breeding in Great Britain. I had a great love (I suppose it was inherent) for birds, and I also was proud to earn a few shillings a week for my dear old mother. So I turned in under the guidance of my brother, who had charge of the aviary, and was put to work at cleaning, feeding, breeding, and generally attending to the parrots—that talkative tropical bird, whose tongue imitates so well the speech of man and woman.

It was, perhaps, the happiest week's work I ever put in, and I assure my readers it was a delightful occupation.

CHAPTER III.

MY EXPERIENCE WITH BIRDS AT KNOWSLEY.

"Feed and tend birds," say you, "a delightful occupation? Oh! I like birds well enough; but then I want the servants, my sister, or mother, to feed and clean after them. I like to see them, and listen to their singing; but I don't care about the bother of attending to their wants." Oh, my dear readers, there's where you miss it. You cannot have the affection of any of the feathered tribe, nor really love the little pets, unless you sacrifice something for them. You must learn how to clean for them, what their various wants are, and you must also study their character to learn their little ways, before you can appreciate them, or they will appreciate you.

To illustrate: When I was crossing the Atlantic with "Jumbo," I had considerable leisure, and loved to be on the quarter-deck to watch the movements of the "sea gulls,' the birds of the sea that followed and hovered around the stern of the ship all day long. I soon made their acquaintance after leaving Queenstown's beautiful bay.

I made a practice of filling my pockets with bread at meal times, and when it was a little more stormy than usual, and no persons were on deck, except the officers on duty, I would have all the birds to myself. They would soar around the after part of the steamship, as majestically as eagles soar in the heavens, and with the eyes of hawks, and the swiftness of falcons, sweep over the turbulent green and white waters which the screw of the ship threw madly up as she ploughed the mighty deep.

Sometimes, as the steamer pitched forward, the screw propeller would come to the surface of the waters, and I tell you, my dear readers, that it required some real nerve to sit on the side of the ship with legs dangling over the side, holding on by my left arm to the rigging, and feeding the birds with the right hand, in a rather rough sea. Yet that was, I found, about as good a place to sit as any other, and somewhat better to view the graceful actions of these birds of the briny deep, as the pretty creatures battled with the wind over the mighty waters, which man has not been fully able to master.

There is only one Master of these elements.

When I was a boy in a Sunday-school, we used to sing the following simple hymn, which a thousand times recurs to my mind.

I think it apropos to introduce it here, as it tells how the waters were mastered only once, and then by the "Great Master."

"A little ship was on the sea,
It was a pretty sight,
It sailed along so pleasantly,
And all was calm and bright.
When lo! a storm began to rise;
The wind blew loud and strong,
It blew the waves across the sky,
It blew the waves along,
And all but One were sore afraid
Of sinking in the deep.
His head was on a pillow laid,
And he was fast asleep.
'Master, we perish; master, save!'
He rose; rebuked the wind and wave,
And stilled them with a word.
And well we know it was the Lord,
Our Saviour and our Friend,
Whose care of those who love his word
Will never, never end."

CHAPTER IV.

MY LIFE AT LORD DERBY'S SEAT, KNOWSLEY, ENGLAND.

But to continue the story of my experiences on the voyage. As I sat in the position heretofore described, I fed these sea-gulls, and the pleasure and delight that filled my soul as the hundreds of birds swooped down from their heights to the surface of the troubled waters was very great. They picked up every crumb, and that without confusion. There was no scrambling for the food, such as was indulged in by the poor two-legged creatures down in the steerage, when the steward pitched his tin of fish or flesh on the floor of the cabin. The bird that first reached a crumb of bread took it up, and the others soared away to take another chance, which I soon gave them. I learned much from these birds in their native element, to be added to my stock of knowledge gathered from them in their imprisoned state in the Gardens at Knowsley, and at the Zoological Gardens, London.

Now, if I had not sacrificed a little comfort, and taken the trouble to feed them, they would not have had the confidence in me which to my mind they plainly exhibited. Nor would I have learned their ways. I could tell the reader a great deal more of the habits of these birds, but lack of space prevents me doing so.

The real lover of the feathered tribes *always* feeds and nurses them. It is a fact that you cannot love, or have the affection of any bird or other animal, without attending to its wants, to some extent.

I was about five years in charge of the parrots at Knowsley, and was very fond of them. In fact, to be candid, I was loth to leave them; but as I had grown into a sharp, active stripling of a lad, as nimble and as athletic as a young panther, I was told to go up higher, and was appointed keeper to those most beautiful and graceful of all animals, the deers and antelopes, as well as some other larger natives of the forest.

I passed several years in this position, growing up into manhood, at times contending actively with the wilder and more unmanageable animals. I have read in the good old Bible of young David having killed the lion, when he was keeping his father's sheep on the plains of Palestine.

My experience teaches me that the statement of David is true, and I can understand how, without any use of miraculous power, the stripling could and did slay the lion. *I know how it is done*, and can do it if necessary, and could have done it when I was a stripling of seventeen years of age. But I would rather heal a sore, take a thorn out of a foot, nurse an animal through inflammation of the bowels, with its disagreeable attending consequences, than I would slay any brute.

But, perhaps, my readers may think this a weakness. However, I respectfully but firmly disagree with you, and take the negative side.

Why, I have nursed "Jumbo," the largest, most intelligent, and certainly the most powerful living animal in creation. He weighs nearly eight tons; he stands to-day nearly twelve feet high in his "bare feet." He can swing by his step, at "walking gait," the largest suspension bridge that man has ever built. He is now at his majority, and ready for all the duties of manhood. He was given to me a baby, and I have been more than a father to him, for I have performed the duties and bestowed the affections of a mother as far as my humble ability would permit. I am proud of my boy, "Jumbo." All the experience shared with him is a pleasure to me, and is a great reward, which I am thankful for in these my older days. I feel them creeping on, but so long as I am permitted the company of dear old Jumbo, I shall be quite contented.

If Jumbo goes on growing to the average age of man, when he arrives at that figure he will be a prodigious monster. I don't know what he will grow into either in mind or instinct (call it what you like).

I know this, that I am happy in his company, and do not wish to leave it. We are close companions, and if he lives until my death I verily believe it will break his heart. If he survives me, I don't know who can possibly associate with him, for ever since I brought him away from his wife Alice, whom we left in England, he has been extremely fractious in his temper even with me, and no one else can venture near him if they value their lives.

But to return to my story.

After I had spent some years in the wild beast department at Knowsley, the old earl died, and we buried him with his fathers.

CHAPTER V.

MY EXPERIENCES IN THE ZOÖLOGICAL SOCIETY'S GARDENS, LONDON—ALSO SOME REMARKS ABOUT A STRANGE BIRD, THE APTERYX.

The Earl had left a legacy to the Zoological Society of London. He left them the choice of any set of animals or birds they might prefer. Strange to say, the Society chose my favorite Eland antelopes, a beautiful set of five natives of South Africa. As they had been under my care for many years, the Society prevailed upon the succeeding Earl (the present Earl's father), to allow me to go with the "Elands" to London. This changed the whole course of my life. I was packed off with the Elands to the greatest city in the world, and entered London in 1851 for the first time, under these very peculiar circumstances.

I lived in London at the Zoölogical Gardens most part of my life (about thirty years), during which time I bred, nursed, and raised more foreign birds and animals than any other living man. I had animals from Asia, Africa, Australia, New Zealand, America, Europe, and, in fact, from all parts of the globe. Especially do I wish to remark that I raised a large number of young Eland antelopes. Indeed, I raised over forty of those graceful creatures myself, as well as watching and tending many other wild animals during the same period.

The first specimens I had the pleasure of breeding and raising at the Zoölogical Gardens were a set of birds called the Cassowary. A family of birds belonging to the ostrich order, natives of India, Mexico, Guiana, and the Brazils. It has a short bill, arch-shaped above the base; the cheeks are almost naked; wattles like a rooster; a helmet on the top of the head. The bird is about the size of a middle-aged ostrich. A dark-brown plumage, a little green shade about the head. When fighting with its enemies it uses its legs in the same manner as a pugilist strikes his antagonist, delivering his blows from the hip, just as a man strikes "right out from the shoulder."

The greatest curiosity of the feathered tribe I am certain, to my mind, is of the ostrich family, and is called the Apteryx, a native of New Zealand.

Of all the feathered tribes that have come within my knowledge perhaps this is the most curious. The covering is half feathers and half hair; the color is dark brown. It is thought by the leading naturalists (and I agree with them), to be the connecting link between the bird and

THE APTERYX.

beast. The proboscis is quite at the end of the beak, which is near a foot in length, and is used for boring into the earth, and also as a suction-pipe to draw up snails and worms from below the surface. On the legs and feet are three toes or claws considerably apart. The average weight of the egg of this bird is fourteen and a half ounces, being one-fourth part of the weight of the "beast-bird" itself.

This "beast-bird" was in the Gardens seven years before it required an ounce of water (although a perfect teetotaller).

One morning I found the Apteryx apparently in a bad state of health, and when I called the attention of the professors and scientific men to its condition they all declared that the bird must be old and used up, and they predicted its death accordingly. I put in a word of appeal for the poor creature. I told the professors that, although not certain, it was my impression the bird was simply breeding and engaged in forming an egg, and that in all probability she was not sick at all.

My observations were ridiculed, and I was laughed at, yet I persevered in standing by my opinion. As in many other instances, my perseverance was at length rewarded by my being allowed to have my own way. I set to work at once and watched and attended to the Apteryx night and day. The sequel proved that my opinion was the correct one, and to my great joy, and no doubt her relief, she delivered herself of an immense egg.

CHAPTER VI.

THE PECULIAR NATURE AND HABITS OF THE APTERYX—THE STRANGEST OF ALL BIRDS.

When the time of delivery was at hand, I supplied her with water, and she used it freely, as a help to deliver the egg. This was the first water she had used in seven years (being a bird of absorption), and until the time of delivery she never required water at all as a drink.

Seventeen days elapsed from the time I got full control of the bird (dating from the day the professors had given her up), when she was safely delivered of the first egg ever laid on the Island of Great Britain, or in any other country or clime, away from her native wilds.

The female Apteryx produces an egg ready for hatching without ever seeing a male bird.

I may inform my reader that when the female bird produces an egg, one or more of the male birds of the family in the neighborhood at the time of its production, assemble and take charge of the egg. If several eggs are laid by different birds, the males collect them together and take charge of them, until the females of the whole colony have done producing and laying eggs for the season. The male birds then proceed to hatch out the eggs.

There was much contradiction and great argument over my statements in regard to this representative of the feathered tribe of New Zealand. The wise men—scientists and naturalists—"sat in council," and asserted that I could not possibly know anything about the breeding and hatching of these birds in their native state, as I had never been out of England. This first egg was considered such a wonder that it was decided to send out to New Zealand and bring over some of the chiefs of the various tribes, in order that something might be learned about the manner of production and hatching out of this egg. The chiefs from the Antipodes came to see this great phenomenon, and pronounced their opinion. When they had given in their verdict, I begged to differ with their views, and expressed myself accordingly, and proved that these savages were simply ignoramuses on the subject. It was then decided to send them back to New Zealand in order to bring over a male bird to hatch out the egg, and after much trouble this was accomplished.

The chiefs returned to New Zealand and obtained and shipped to England a male Apteryx. On its arrival he was shown, and immediately took to sitting on and hatching out the egg laid by my female bird. During the time this male bird from New Zealand was sitting on the first egg of my pet Apteryx, he died suddenly, and there was a great investigation as to the cause, but no definite information was gleaned at the time. I carefully examined this dead Apteryx, and although I was not allowed to make a post-mortem examination, I found out the cause. There were a great many mice about the place, and I discovered that they had attacked him while he was sitting on the egg and eaten through his skin and flesh to the bone. No doubt this took away his life. I have never known, heard, or read of greater or more devoted duty on the part of any of God's creatures than was displayed by this male Apteryx, a stranger from New Zealand, a prisoner, faithfully and tenderly doing the duty nature had ordained it to do, and that even when its vitals were being gnawed out. Such bravery is seldom met with. I may be pardoned for bringing this seeming trivial thing to the notice and for the benefit of my readers. Of course, the eggs of my pet bird were never hatched out, and I was a greatly disappointed man.

During the long spell my pet bird was breeding she was also awfully bitten by mice; the mice had made one considerable hole in the under part of her body. I had done all I could, used all my ingenuity, and tried all the ways and means of destroying the vermin, but as I dared not use poison I found it impossible to trap and catch them all. I nursed my pet bird with that care and thought I had many other animals and birds (I think even more so), and was rewarded by having her life saved.

The Apteryx is, to my knowledge, the most curious bird I have ever had to do with in my long experience.

CHAPTER VII.

MORE ABOUT THE APTERYX AND OSTRICH TRIBE GENERALLY.

The Apteryx produces only two eggs in a season. The first young Apteryx hatched out accompanies the female bird, its mother, during the time the male bird is hatching out the second egg. They then all join as one happy family, and journey along through life together.

The most remarkable feature of the habits of this bird, is that the female conceives, breeds, and produces the egg without the aid of the male bird—as remarked before.

The Apteryx is a nocturnal bird. It sleeps all day and takes its pleasures and hunts for food by night.

I have watched my Apteryx often when she went about in the dark seeking her food, boring down into the ground with her long bill for worms, snails, and such small fry. Then I have seen her, after she had filled her stomach with food, take her ease and comfort. Really, my dear readers, I cannot find words to tell you what pleasure I took in seeing that bird roam about at night when all nature seemed to be reposing, while she sang and enjoyed herself. She made a peculiar sound, something like "kawo," "kawo," "kawo," clear and shrill, and as I sat smoking my pipe and watching her, I tell you it was something fine to see how happy this bird of the night was. It reminded me of the nightingale, which, as everybody knows, sings at night. The male Apteryx had more of a whistling sound than the female.

We have often heard and read of the travellers in the East and South, where these ostrich tribes live and flourish in their native element, that the birds lay their eggs in the sand, and leave them there to be hatched out by the heat of the sun. It is not so. The sun is not always shining, nor can there always be the same temperature. To produce young from eggs the temperature must be about the same during the twenty-four hours. All chicken breeders by steam or other artificial heat know this.

The fact is, the female bird lays her egg in the sand where she is at the time of delivery, and immediately the male bird in the vicinity at such time takes possession, and sits on the egg, never deserting it except when compelled to travel in quest of food, and then only for a very short time.

CHAPTER VIII.

THE LANDSEER MEDAL, PRESENTED TO ME BY THE ZOÖLOGICAL SOCIETY, LONDON, 1866 —CONCLUSION OF AUTOBIOGRAPHY.

I have indulged in a more detailed description of the Cassowary and Apteryx, than what I intended giving; but the latter is such a very rare and strange bird, that I thought it better to acquaint my readers with its peculiarities. They are indeed peculiar; so much so, that the naturalists and scientists of the greatest zoölogical collection in the world were completely at sea in reference to them. The experiences, as told, prove this; and I flatter-myself that my care and observation of the bird have added a valuable page to natural history.

I shall soon conclude my humble autobiography.

After many years of varied experience, the naturalists and members of the Zoölogical Society, London, without a single exception, united in presenting me with a set of resolutions in 1866. They accompanied a magnificent bronze medal, of which I am justly, I think, proud. The medal was designed by no less an artist than Sir Edwin Landseer, the greatest animal painter that ever lived.

The designs are beautifully executed. One side represents the beasts, viz.: the elephant, rhinoceros, giraffe, Hindoo bull, llama, etc. The other side represents the birds, as follows: the eagle, ostrich, crane, adjutant, pelican, condor, swan, parrot, stork, ibis, and bird of paradise. (See engravings in front of book.)

The inscription on the medal is as follows:

"To MATTHEW SCOTT, for his success in breeding Foreign Animals, in the Zoölogical Society's Gardens, London, 1866."

I think that the above speaks for itself, and needs no further comment.

The contents of the resolutions were, if possible, more flattering, and modesty prevents my giving them *verbatim.*

I felt, after I was the recipient of both of these testimonials to my humble abilities, that I was rewarded fully for my trials, dangers, and toils, as the care-taker and breeder of the beast and bird. I had but one regret, and that was that my good old mother was not living at the time, to share my pleasure.

I continued in the Gardens, superintending the general management, as to keeping and breeding, until the special task was allotted to me of going to France, to bring over the animal that was destined to become the "animal of animals," viz.: his majesty "Jumbo."

My experiences with him, so varied and peculiar, would fill volumes; but I have endeavored to give some of the salient points of his character, and stories of his wanderings in the "Biography of Jumbo," which follows this.

I am at the present time writing this sketch at Barnum's famous "Winter Quarters," Bridgeport, Conn., and Jumbo is looking down with his wisest air at me. I am quite contented, and so is he. Up to the present time the foregoing takes in a short account of my career. The future is a sealed book; but I fear no danger, for we are all in the care of Him who marks even the sparrow's fall—as I have remarked before. MATTHEW SCOTT.

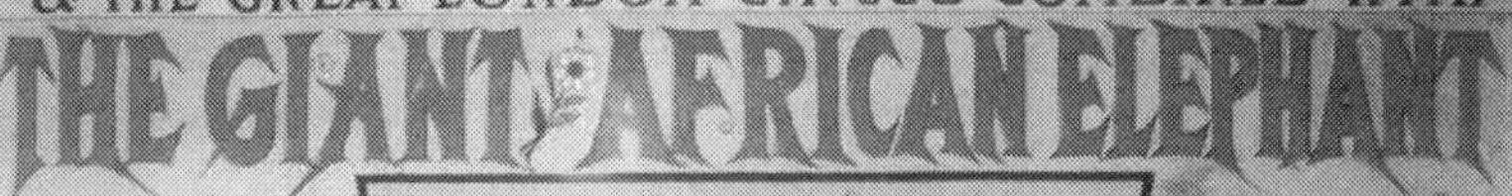

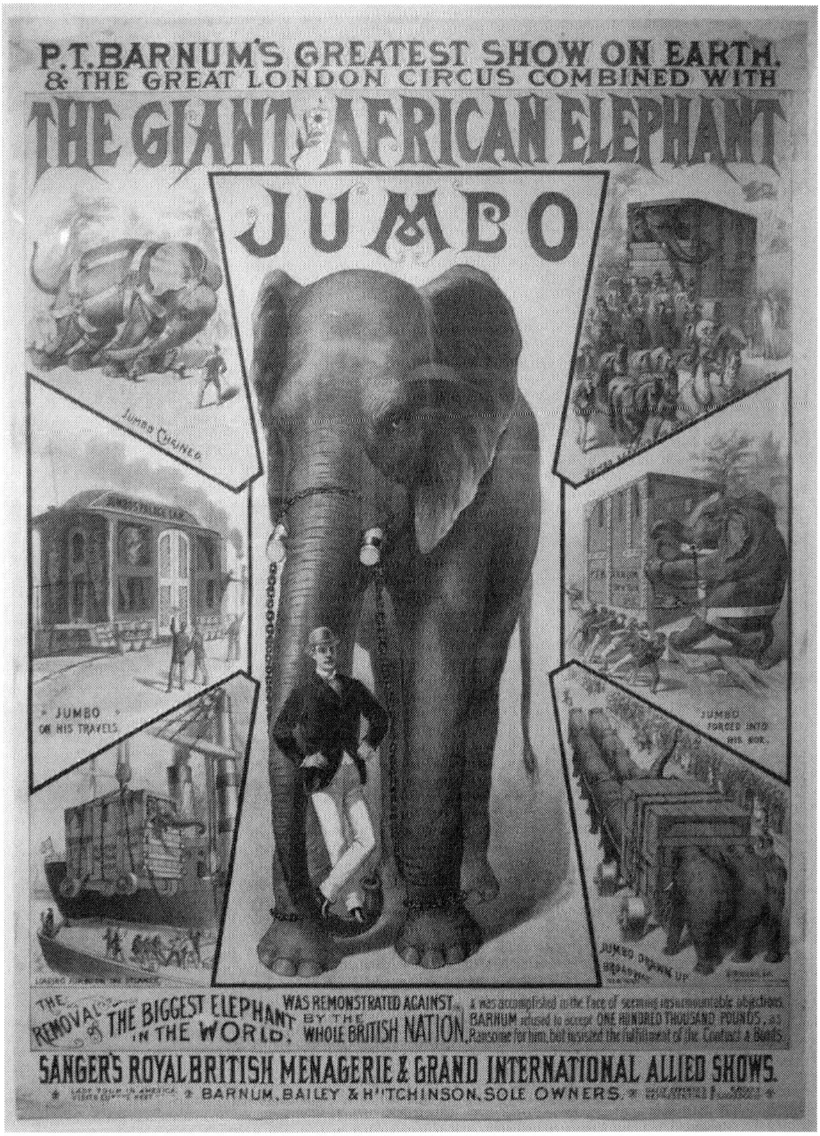
P.T. BARNUM'S GREATEST SHOW ON EARTH.
& THE GREAT LONDON CIRCUS COMBINED WITH
THE GIANT AFRICAN ELEPHANT
JUMBO
JUMBO CHAINED
JUMBO ON HIS TRAVELS.
JUMBO FORCED INTO HIS BOX.
JUMBO DRAWN UP BROADWAY
THE REMOVAL OF THE BIGGEST ELEPHANT IN THE WORLD, WAS REMONSTRATED AGAINST BY THE WHOLE BRITISH NATION.
BARNUM refused to accept ONE HUNDRED THOUSAND POUNDS, as Ransome for him, but insisted the fulfilment of the Contract & Bonds.
SANGER'S ROYAL BRITISH MENAGERIE & GRAND INTERNATIONAL ALLIED SHOWS.
BARNUM, BAILEY & HUTCHINSON, SOLE OWNERS.

JUMBO'S BIOGRAPHY.

BY HIS KEEPER AND FRIEND,

MATTHEW SCOTT.

CHAPTER I.

JUMBO'S FIRST APPEARANCE AT THE ZOÖLOGICAL GARDENS, LONDON.

In writing these chapters the reader will pardon me, no doubt, should I display any seeming eccentricity, so to speak, or if I depart from the ordinary mode of book-making.

As this is not written for mercenary purposes or financial reward, I think you will perhaps indulge me in whatever may seem peculiar. I shall, like Othello, "Nothing extenuate nor aught set down in malice, but a round unvarnished tale deliver."

The first object that moves me to write this is for the glory of God, the giver of all good. The second, to benefit the people of the United States of America and Great Britain, in both of which countries I have been received from shore to shore with the greatest kindness, and Jumbo with the most unbounded enthusiasm. It is to me a joy and satisfaction also to give out the knowledge I possess, and display before the world God's great goodness, love, and affection manifested in not only the human family, but in everything, and to *prove* that the Giver and Provider from whom only all good comes, notes all things. And because, as was said by a worthy divine in an Episcopal church last Sunday night, "Whatever makes known and discloses a knowledge of God to the extent of becoming an instrument of good and benefit to any of God's creatures, displays God in his own person for the benefit of the world, thereby being a power and antidote to all disease and evil, both to the human-family and the brute creation."

When I first saw Jumbo I met him on the coast of France. He was about being brought from that country to England for medical care—to your humble servant, the animals' physician. A more deplorable, diseased, and rotten creature never walked God's earth, to my knowledge. Jumbo had been presented to France, together with another baby elephant, when they were quite infants.

When he was given in my charge, outside of Paris, his condition was simply filthy. He had been in the care of Frenchmen for several years, and they either did not know how to treat the race of elephants, or culpably neglected his raising. I don't know which, but when I met him in France I thought I never saw a creature so woe-begone. The poor thing was full of disease, which had worked its way through the animal's hide, and had almost eaten out its eyes. The hoofs of the feet and the tail were literally rotten, and the whole hide was so covered with sores, that the only thing I can compare it to was the condition of the man of leprosy spoken of in the good old "Guide-book," or of Job's state, when he had to scrape himself with a potsherd. However, I received Jumbo as I have received many other of God's creatures that other people have given up for "a bad job." I received him kindly, took him tenderly over the Channel, and lodged him in a comfortable, clean bed in my stable. I undertook to be his doctor, his nurse, and general servant. I watched and nursed him night and day with all the care and affection of a mother (if it were possible for a man to do such a thing), until by physicking from the inward centre of his frame I cleared out all diseased matter from his lungs, liver, and heart. I then, by means of lotions of oil, etc., took all the scabs from the roots of his almost blinded eyes. I removed his leprous coat as cleanly as a man takes off an overcoat; and his skin was as fine as that of a horse just from the clipper's, after the hair had been cut off. I was rewarded by having a clean-shaven looking creature in a perfectly sound state of mind and body; and he required no blanket nor overcoat, although he was far,

far from home, in a much more northerly climate than his native element in "Afric's Sunny Sands." Taking climate and covering into account, it was like transferring a man from the western shores of the Atlantic to "Greenland's Icy Mountains."

CHAPTER II.

JUMBO'S COMPANION ELEPHANT ALICE, AT THE ZOÖLOGICAL GARDENS, LONDON.

Her name is Alice. She is a native of the west coast of Africa, and was born in the year of our Lord one thousand eight hundred and sixty-four, the same year that Jumbo—nearly four years old—was brought to me.

She was born in the midst of a tribe of wild elephants that roamed about and sported in the freedom of their native element in the region spoken of above.

When Jumbo had grown into a good-sized Elephant Boy, I suggested that we ought to get him a sweetheart, so that, although he was a prisoner, chained and manacled in the Zoölogical Gardens, London, he would have a companion through life of his own race. So, having Jumbo entirely under my own care and management, I persuaded our Garden Directors to send to Africa for a female baby elephant. I must say the Directors were very good to me, at that time. They saw that I had got a fine specimen of the elephant tribe in my Jumbo, and that he was going to beat the world as a curiosity and wonder—which the sequel has proved.

So they sent ambassadors all the way to Africa, with instructions to buy or capture a good specimen of the female baby elephant.

These men went down from London to the great sea, and arriving on the west coast of Africa, after considerable search, found such a specimen as they thought would answer my purpose. They brought it over safely and deposited it in my care and keeping.

The arrival of this female baby elephant—not a year old—caused me great joy, and I cannot find words to express to my readers the pleasure and happiness I experienced at beholding my Jumbo's delight when he first saw Alice coming along. Jumbo was now about four years old, and I stood head and shoulders above him in height.

If I could have the pleasure of that day over again, I would make a considerable sacrifice. However, when I passed by Jumbo's stable, where he roamed at leisure, the moment he saw Alice led along toward him, I thought he would have broken that stable front out to get at us. His delight and pleasure, expressed in the liveliest manner possible, and which I understood, exceeded that of any boy when he meets his sweetheart for the first time. At least my Jumbo was more demonstrative and, I verily believe, possessed more real affection and love at first sight than most of the young men of the present generation do in a like situation. Jumbo's great antics on this occasion were very entertaining, and if I may be pardoned for saying so much about these dear children of the forest, it did me good to behold them at the time, and even now I am happy in recapitulating the circumstances.

I immediately associated the young female elephant with Jumbo in a separate stall. We named her Alice; he was very proud of his sweetheart, and continued to cut great capers for quite a time.

Jumbo always showed the greatest regard for Alice, a good deal more so in fact than some young men show for their sweethearts in this or any other country.

Jumbo and Alice lived very happily together in the Zoölogical Gardens, London, for about seventeen years, and want of space prevents me from telling of the numerous interesting events that came within my knowledge as I tended and raised these young folks through their childhood to man and woman's estate, so to speak. But I will observe, before leaving this part of the subject of Alice's history, that I never, in all my experience among animals or humanity, saw more respect, deference, and affection shown by a male to a female than Jumbo paid at all times to Alice, even during his sickness. And in return, he received that true feminine affection and devotion from Alice which characterizes all true daughters of man or beast since the days of Adam and Eve. Nay, I will go further, I don't think that Alice ever deceived Jumbo; she certainly never flirted with any other elephants (and she often had the chance).

CHAPTER III.

JUMBO AS A SWIMMER.

Jumbo knows how to bathe and swim; I may say he is a "great swimmer." He makes a bigger hole in the water than most other animals, and he certainly throws water up into the air higher than any other animal, with his great water-spout trunk.

When in London some years ago, it being inconvenient to take Jumbo down to the river, it was arranged to construct a special bath for him and Alice, his wife. I just wish I had the boys and girls who have done so much shouting for Jumbo in this country, with me there to see Jumbo and Alice bathing. I would not wish for greater pleasure than to stand upon the top of the bath and look into their faces as they would gaze with intensity at the manœuvres of Jumbo as he led the way into the bath, down to the deep end, where he could have a swim, with Alice close at his heels. It is impossible to describe the amusing scene.

Jumbo would, every now and then, turn right about and with his massive trunk throw up such a quantity of water as would make a shower-bath fall on Alice's back, and then, perhaps, he would in the same way, throw up to a great height a regular three-inch water-pipe gush of a douche bath, and this would so tickle Alice, and so add to her enjoyment, that she would presently begin to reciprocate; but as her trunk and powers were not so great as Jumbo's, she could not make such a good job of it. Yet Jumbo was awfully pleased at Alice's consideration in trying thus to wash his back. Jumbo would make a good five- or six-story window-washer.

When they got to swimming depth they would play some of the funniest frolics, rolling about like two ships in a storm at sea; and at other times would swim most majestically along, Jumbo always leading the way for quite a time, then, when they got to the end of the oblong bath, Alice would turn round and Jumbo would follow her back to walking depth; then some more shower-bath business, and after that a return for a few dives. It is really amusing to see Jumbo on his head trying to show his hind legs, just like the boys do when they are bathing.

Jumbo and I had the same kind of fun out West in the rivers, whenever we had an opportunity, the only difference being that I had to take Alice's place. I got all the shower and douche bath without the ability to return the kindness. Being without a long water-spout of a trunk, I couldn't do more than splash a bit with my hands, or throw a few buckets of water on Jumbo's back, and although he appreciated my efforts as a substitute, he never has enjoyed his bath as much as he did when Alice was along with him.

Jumbo is a remarkably clean animal, and he is mighty particular about his bed, and, indeed, in all his habits he is a model of cleanliness.

CHAPTER IV.

JUMBO'S BUSY LIFE AT THE ZOÖLOGICAL GARDENS, AND HIS LOVE FOR LITTLE CHILDREN.

Jumbo has had a busy life. I would tell my young readers that, as Mrs. General Garfield once said, "a busy life is the happiest." That good and noble lady once wrote to our late worthy President, and told him her happiest thoughts came to her when she was busy "baking the nice white bread" and thinking of her dear noble husband, who was also busy "all the way through," from the time he drove the boat horse on the canal bank, up to the time he embraced his good old mother in the presence of thousands of his country's representatives at Washington, during the scene of his inauguration.

Jumbo, I say, has been a busy, industrious creature all his life, especially since I brought him from his sick bed. He is like many a noble-minded man, who has been stricken down with sickness and raised up again, like old Job, to bless and magnify his creator. Jumbo has had no idle days for "loafing" or hanging around stores or otherwise wasting his time. He has been engaged in carrying around the children of the human family almost daily for twenty years, and I suppose no animal has ever carried so many on his back as Jumbo. Certainly I can claim for him that no animal ever did his work more affectionately or tenderly, and freer from accident.

Once when I was riding him around in the Zoölogical Gardens, in London, sitting on his neck, with about a dozen children on a panier-saddle across his broad back, we were proceeding down the path. It was on a delightful summer afternoon, and the grass plots, flowers, plants, and trees, which abound in those magnificent gardens, looked beautiful. I was engaged talking to the dozen "little folk" who occupied his back, and encouraging them to sit very quietly and not fall off, when all at once Master Jumbo came to a standstill for some cause or other. I shouted to him to go along, but for once he did not obey the order. As I turned round to see what was the matter, there was a lady running over the grass-plot on to the path, screaming and shouting, "Oh, my poor child! my child, my child! oh, he will be killed, he will be killed!"

Well, I looked down from my elevation and saw Jumbo deliberately and coolly putting his trunk around the body of an infant that escaped its mother's apron-strings and had run and fallen in front of Jumbo. Jumbo is a very careful walker, and always looks where he is going, and, like some others of God's creatures, is rather slow in his movements, but both very sure-footed and thoughtful. He just stopped right there, gently picked up the child by the waist with his trunk, and laid it on the green grass beside its screaming mother, more tenderly than the mother afterward took up the frightened child in her excitement.

Jumbo never gets excited when he is attending to children. He might get mad once in a while, when some drunken fool tries to prick him with pins stuck in a cake, or otherwise fool him. Jumbo always knows parties that try to play tricks upon him when he is being exhibited to the masses of humanity, and if ever any of such parties should come within the reach of Jumbo a second time it wouldn't be good for him. A woman would not do a dirty trick to Jumbo.

Now, my dear young boys, let me tell you that Jumbo was only ten years old at this time, and I want you to see right here the great lesson taught by Jumbo in this tender action: to always be kind, loving, and helpful to your little sisters when you see them fall down or hurt themselves, and, if you learn to carry this into practice, this trivial incident of God's wisdom, through one of his creatures, will be a blessed and profitable habit all through life, and your friend and Jumbo will be fully rewarded.

I want you to think of Jumbo as a kind,

affectionate creature; never mind his being an awkward, overgrown "old boy;" don't look at the exterior so much. "Fine feathers make fine birds," is an old saying, but remember, when you see a little girl anyway in trouble, you should go instantly to the rescue, and remember that poor Jumbo did the same thing.

CHAPTER V.

JUMBO'S FONDNESS FOR MUSIC AND HIS KEEPER.

I must tell you that all his life, from the time I raised him from the bed—that was thought by most people that saw him in the diseased state I have described would be his death-bed — up to the present time, he has been a great lover of music. I don't mean that he is very musical himself, as a vocalist or player on any instrument, but he is a very fair and appreciative creature. For instance, when at the Zoological Gardens, London, we had the grand band of the "Horse Guards" playing in the grounds every week; and when, as was occasionally the case, the men were away on duty elsewhere, another band was engaged, Master Jumbo knew the difference, although he could not always see the musicians.

He was so fond of the "Horse Guards," and the boys were so fond of him, that they were always good friends, and Jumbo knew at once when any other band struck up a tune, and he would soon *let me know* that the hired band wasn't his favorite "Horse Guards'" Band.

I dare say that there are many boys now

of only the age that Jumbo was at that time, who would not be able to distinguish the difference in the music under the same circumstances.

I ought, perhaps, to tell my young readers that Jumbo has had, and even has to-day some habits that are rather babyish. I suppose you, my readers, and I have our faults and failings, like all other intelligent and instinctive animals; and one of Jumbo's faults is that when I am out of his sight, or rather when I go away, he knows it, and if I don't come back at regular times he always makes me aware of it, both day and night. And he is selfish, for if I am an hour or two overdue after the time he is looking for me, he commences to whine and cry, and becomes very naughty, just the same as a child crying after its mother. Not that he wants anything but my company. However, you will forgive him. Won't you? As you remember you have done the same thing yourselves. So learn to be charitable and forgiving to others.

It was thought by the people of England that Jumbo could not be brought to see the American nation. It was held—and a good deal of pressure was brought to bear upon me, to the effect—that I should never be able to make the voyage across the Atlantic in safety with so monstrous an animal, and that the risk anyway was too great. It was also held by some that, as there were thousands of Americans coming to London every season, it was too risky a speculation or enterprise to pay, as the most of such visitors would have seen Jumbo in London.

I am sometimes tickled a bit, when I think

of the tens of thousands of miles Jumbo and I have travelled in the interior of this country since we made the perilous journey of three thousand miles by sea to the American shores; and I often wonder what the people of the old country will say to me when they hear of our travels out West, North, and South, or what they will say to me when we get back to our own shores.

CHAPTER VI.

ARRANGEMENTS MADE BY MR. P. T. BARNUM, "THE GREATEST SHOWMAN ON EARTH," TO EXHIBIT JUMBO IN THE UNITED STATES.

When, in the year 1882, Mr. P. T. Barnum, "The Greatest Showman on Earth," had completed all arrangements for the exhibition of Jumbo to the people of the

United States, I consented, after considerable persuasion, to accompany him on his voyage across the broad Atlantic, and to exhibit him to the American nation, then numbering nearly fifty millions of souls. One of the reasons which persuaded me was that I anticipated meeting again many kind old friends who had left the Old Country for the New, and had become happy and prosperous under the "starry banner." I must confess that I was somewhat curious to see what kind of reception would be accorded Jumbo. I was not at all anxious, for I felt he would make a great sensation, but curious to see how he would be received in a strange land. I may add that I have not been disappointed. On the contrary, I and Jumbo have received the utmost courtesy, and the kindest hospitality wherever we have been, and on our great western "ten-thousand-miles tour" in the far west Jumbo has been received, applauded, and what I value most, *appreciated* by the free sons of toil who are clearing the finest country under the sun. The ovations have been something beyond my most sanguine expectations, and I am grateful to the American people for their reception of Jumbo.

General Tom Thumb acknowledged, when he visited us at Brockton, Mass., that Jumbo was "a bigger card" than himself. Well, this was amusing, coming from the smallest man, and yet a man who, perhaps, had the biggest record for sight-seeing on earth.

CHAPTER VII.

JUMBO'S DEEP GRIEF ON PARTING WITH HIS WIFE ALICE.

It was one thing to propose and another thing to dispose of the difficulty in the case of parting Jumbo from Alice.

The parting of Uncle Tom from his negro wife, down in "Old Kentucky," when he was sold in the slave-market, was nothing to it.

I never thought it would be such a job. However, it had to be done. I had given my word — and that is my bond — and Jumbo and I always carry out that principle whatever the cost.

Mr. P. T. Barnum, "the greatest showman on earth," had made arrangements, and had promised to exhibit Jumbo to the Americans.

We took steps to tear those poor slaves apart, and it was no small matter, and I want you, my readers, to let me tell you my views on this subject:

When the time came for sundering Jumbo and Alice, the actions of Alice, in the movements of her body and the horrible groans, were something awful to listen to. And I assure you that no parent, seeing his son and daughter sold to separate owners in the slave-market of South Carolina, and torn apart, one to go to one place and the other to another, could have suffered more heart-rending pain and fear than my soul underwent on that occasion.

The noise of the groans of Alice was at times of a wailing, plaintive, rather musical kind. Then it would sound like the roar of thunder, and at times was as quick and successive as its peals. She tore about the stable in which she was confined, and dashed herself against its sides, till we expected every minute she would break loose and follow us. If she had, we should have had a nice time of it to separate them again. I hold that Jumbo and Alice could walk this earth in company and hold their own, and even with my friendly and familiar voice, I question, without great strength and force, whether they could have been separated again. Certainly they could not have been parted without injury to them.

We ultimately got Jumbo away from her, and for a considerable time after we left, poor Alice was a very dejected and despondent animal; she has never been the same since, and she never will be until I take her husband, Jumbo, back to her, which I purpose by God's help doing, as well for the peace of my own mind as the pleasure and satisfaction of the two sweethearts. I can then, I hope, finish my bachelor life in company with my two "little" pets. If this cannot be done, I shall insist upon the only other alternative, that is, to bring Alice over to the American Continent, and so reunite them on American soil.

It does not trouble me which plan is adopted. But one thing I have determined in my own mind shall be done; that is, that Jumbo and Alice must and shall be reunited; it is a wrong and a sin to keep them apart, especially as they cannot cable, telephone, or otherwise correspond, like the human family.

CHAPTER VIII.

JUMBO'S DEPARTURE FROM ENGLAND AND VOYAGE TO THE UNITED STATES.

When the English public was informed of Jumbo's intended departure loud protests were raised. The feeling was intense, and the people were so earnest and determined that Jumbo should not leave England, that a proposition was made to raise by subscription from the masses, a sufficient sum of money to buy him from the Zoölogical Society.

Elaborate preparations were made for Jumbo's shipment. A large box, made of the strongest oak, and as big as a small house, was constructed for him, to be used from the Gardens until he arrived in the United States. It was furnished with every comfort that could appeal to Jumbo's luxurious tastes.

Strange to say, "his majesty" did not seem to appreciate it, for when we invited him to enter he vigorously refused. We tried to get him in again and again during two days, and succeeded only on the third in doing so. We fastened him in securely, leaving only a space or hole in the top of the front, through which he could see and flourish his trunk.

In the dawn of a fine spring morning we started on our journey to the New World. The box was drawn by sixteen horses, and the weight was as much as they could draw. Thousands followed Jumbo to the river-bank, expressing their regrets at his departure. The grief of the children was really sorrowful.

At Gravesend Jumbo held a levee, and

a very fashionable one too, for a distinguished company came on board the steamer to wish him *bon voyage*. Among the party were Miss Burdett-Coutts, and her present husband; also Mr. Henry Irving, the great actor, and several other well-known ladies and gentlemen.

One poor old lady gave me several cakes and bottles of soda water to be given to Jumbo on the passage.

Jumbo was somewhat alarmed at first by the noise of the machinery and the rolling of the steamship; but I was always at his side, and managed to calm him so that he became quite a sailor when he got his sea legs on.

We arrived at last, and Jumbo seemed to be delighted. He trumpeted out his joy, as much as to say, "Ah! Mr. Scott, we are at last in the 'land of the free and the home of the brave.'" When Jumbo's house was hoisted on the dock ten horses were hitched to the car upon which it was placed. Then two of his brother elephants, called "pushers," put their immense heads to the back of the house, and at a signal the horses commenced to draw and the elephants to push; and after an hour's work we arrived at Madison Square Garden, where Jumbo was released from his narrow quarters, and seemed so joyful at his freedom that he twined his trunk around me in an ecstasy of delight.

CHAPTER IX.

JUMBO'S HABITS, GOOD AND BAD, AND HIS GREAT POPULARITY.

I beg in all modesty to state that Jumbo instinctively is as intelligent and sensitive on all matters pertaining to his race as the average young man or maiden of the same time of life. Let me with all modesty illustrate: Jumbo is very regular in his diet and all the habits of life —he never drinks liquor or aught else before eating; he never drinks while he is "breaking" or masticating his food.

Jumbo's diet is composed of hay, oats, beans, onions, cabbages, beetroot, and bread; his drink is chiefly water and *medicinally* he can stand a big dram of whiskey.

Jumbo's sleeping hours are not near so good when chained up as when he is loose and at liberty to exercise himself. He worries and chafes at being chained by the leg, and, like all other creatures, prefers his liberty, and is much happier, as well as healthier, when at large.

I have considerable difficulty with Jumbo when travelling on the steam cars, for then Jumbo is like the dog in the manger. He can neither sleep himself, nor will he let me sleep. The shaking and jar of the train, the worrying noises, etc., keep him in a constant ferment of nervous excitement, and he gives me little chance for sleep. I no sooner get just nicely off into a dose than his trunk is groping into my little bed, feeling all round my body to find my face, to ascertain if I am there, so as to awake me to talk to him. Sometimes he is so fidgety during the night that neither of us get any sleep at all. Jumbo gets worried by this mode of travelling to such an extent that if I do not get up to talk to him when he calls me, as above described, he begins to lash his trunk against the sides of the car, and to save the car from being broken to pieces I have to get up and play with and talk to him.

He drinks when he wants to, and, although he is held fast by a cable to the earth a large portion of his time, he has sufficient sense or instinct to tell me when he wants a drink of water. Jumbo is a great "teetotaler," and if my temperance friends want a powerful illustration of a good, healthy, strong, and most powerful frame that practises habits of temperance, either on the "alcohol business" or any other of the many intemperate ways of man and beast, they may refer to my Jumbo as a specimen. And they will not make the reference in vain, for I may observe that the youth of this country and Great Britain, as well as many other countries, are familiar with Jumbo, they having seen him and shouted praises to him with all their dear young hearts; why, the world has no idea of the joy and happiness I have experienced, as I have marched along through the masses of the human family, listening to the praises of the "shouting young fry" of all lands when Jumbo passed along. If I may be pardoned, and I say it with all reverence and humility, the shouting at Jerusalem for the "Son of Man," when he rode triumphantly on an ass, could not have exceeded the shout that has gone up from the children of the United States, as they have watched and waited long hours to get a sight of Jumbo as he has left the "greatest show on earth," and marched down to the dock or to the railway station in the different towns and cities of the United States; why, I have seen them by thousands, when they couldn't find fifty cents to get into the show, ready to pay a quarter of a dollar to just go inside and have one peep at Jumbo. "It's all we want to see, and we wont look at anything else; we don't care about the balance, but oh! let us see Jumbo." My heart has often been pained when I have seen these struggling crowds crying out for a peep at the finest and most intelligent animal the world has ever seen, and when I have led him forth down the road to the depot my heart was made glad and thankful that Jumbo was appreciated, praised, and shouted for. Sometimes it was a perfect ovation. The people with upturned faces would look on, and with flowing handkerchiefs and throats almost rent with effort they would call out, "Here's Jumbo! here's Jumbo!" "Hello, Jumbo!" "Welcome, Jumbo! you're a greater wonder than what we expected, Jumbo." "Good-by, dear old Jumbo!" "We shan't see you again, Jumbo!"

I meant to say before this that Jumbo heartily hates and abominates rats, and it is no wonder, for when he was young and weak, after coming to my care, he was almost devoured by them. Very often in the dead of night I have been awakened by poor Jumbo's groans, as if in pain and trouble, and, when I hastened to see what was the matter, I have beheld the rats by hundreds gnawing his hoofs, and snapping viciously at his legs and tail. In my rage, I have often, with the aid of my good short stick, and by the light of a bull's-eye lantern, slaughtered them by the score. This method I found did not check them. So I put my inventive faculties to work, and made a peculiar, though simple, trap that soon cleaned out the rodents. Jumbo really seemed to thank me for the deliverance, judging by his affectionate antics.

CHAPTER X.

ACCIDENTS CAUSED HIS KEEPER BY JUMBO; ALSO, HOW HE SAVED HIS KEEPER'S LIFE.

Once after arriving at Jersey City from the West on the steam cars, from which place we were about to go by float to Brooklyn, we had to be shunted off the main line onto a switch to let the mail train pass. I was in Jumbo's car, and he was standing up, I was on the off side from the train, about the middle of Jumbo's body, when up came the puffing locomotive, snorting and whistling, rushing past from behind, and as Jumbo could not turn around in his car to see what was up, he just gave one lurch from the train side when the steam went through the grating of his car, and came over, catching me quite tightly between his side and the side of the car. He gave me such a squeeze that I don't want any more like it. I have always been on my guard ever since. I was slightly hurt, but it was not of much consequence.

This occurred at first when we commenced riding in steam cars, a thing Jumbo and I were not used to.

Jumbo was awfully sorry, and grieved over my absence like a little girl left without its mamma in the company of strangers.

On our way from the city of New York, going down to the boat, Jumbo somehow or other put his forefoot down on my big toe and smashed it. I am inclined to think it was my own fault, as I was gazing about me, admiring the immense crowds that were swaying to and fro on each side of us, hardly leaving room to walk, and I suppose my attention being for the moment engaged I probably put my toe under his foot. He couldn't say, "you should put your feet in your pocket," but he looked awfully annoyed at himself as he saw me limping along, and, when I looked up at him, his eyes said more than an ample apology from a human being.

Last year in our winter quarters I was busy making Jumbo's bed, when he, trying to move around so that I could fix things nice, gave a tug at the immense cable by which he is chained to the earth, a tug that cut my shin bone. I thought for the moment my leg was broken, but it turned out merely a severe gash, which did not necessitate my leaving him.

On this occasion Jumbo turned round on hearing my exclamation of pain, and as much as said, "What's up now?" Jumbo knew he had not touched me, and of course he never saw the chain strike me, as he had his back to me.

I have told my readers of the various accidents which happened to me in Jumbo's company, and now, in justice to Jumbo, I shall tell you of how he repaid me for all the suffering he has ever caused me by saving my life, and doubtless the lives of many others.

The incident occurred in Ottumwa, Iowa, on October 16, 1883 (I shall never forget that date). It was just after the tents had been erected, and everything was arranged in order for the afternoon performance. Crowds of people were already in the main tent, while hundreds beseiged the ticket-office. I was in Jumbo's special tent, when all at once a noise, like the bursting of a thunder-storm, caused me to look around in alarm. It was made by thirty elephants stampeding. They had broken their chains and were smashing everything in their way. In a moment they rushed into our tent. If death ever stared me in the face, it did at that moment. On came the black mass of mad animals, and I thought there was no escape from being crushed beneath their heavy feet, when Jumbo came to the rescue.

He twined his trunk about my body like a flash, and placed me out of harm's way between his legs; then stood firmly and stretched out his trunk, as rigid as the limb of a large tree, and permitted not an elephant to get past it. Again and again the crowd of maddened creatures tried to force its way, but Jumbo remained firm and determined until the keepers secured the entire lot. Had Jumbo not prevented the elephants from going out of the enclosure, the loss of life would no doubt have been great.

CHAPTER XI.

JUMBO'S TRIP OVER THE GREAT BROOKLYN BRIDGE—DESCRIPTION OF THE STRUCTURE, ETC.

I had a great feat to perform in New York City the second year after our arrival in America. I must inform my readers in America and Great Britain that the greatest bridge in the world is the bridge over the East River, which empties, through a very deep channel, into the bay of New York. This bridge connects the cities of Brooklyn and New York. It has a span of nearly sixteen hundred feet, suspended by four metallic cables, made of twenty thousand miles of steel wire. The height of roadway is one hundred and twenty feet from the river level at high water.

I was invited to take Jumbo for a processional walk over the great Brooklyn Bridge so as to test its strength. Of course "the greatest showman of the earth"—Mr. P. T. Barnum—had a business object in view; but even he, with his vast and comprehensive mind, hardly realized the grandeur of the show he was about to give to the thousands and tens of thousands of the people of the United States—*Jumbo, the largest known animal in creation, walking on the best and finest promenade in the world.*

Every available space on the tops of the towers and other high places of advantage, as well as on the banks of the river, was covered by thousands upon thousands of human beings, of all kinds and colors, and from all climes, gazing upon the greatest and most sublime works of man and God —the like of which, in my humble judgment, has never before been seen on earth —surpassing, in many respects, the mighty pyramids of Egypt, the handiwork of the ancient world; and showing, to my mind, not only the wonderful skill of the human race, but also the power, wisdom, and goodness of the "Great Architect of the Universe."

I had my doubts about the experiment of marching Jumbo over this great structure. I calculated that if I could coax him into keeping up regular marching order I might possibly get through the performance with safety, but then I also knew if he would commence any of his antics up aloft on that bridge, and begin to dance a hornpipe, so to speak, I expected he would shake the whole concern down into the river.

My readers may not readily understand what is meant here, so I will explain a little. If you will think for a moment you will see that when Jumbo put his foot down on the bridge, as he marched along from New York to Brooklyn, the bridge rebounded after the shock given by his foot. The rebound was met by his second footstep, and there was a great vibration caused by it.

I am said to have a pretty strong nerve, but it was something terrible to feel that vibration as we walked quietly along the promenade of .the bridge. I assure my reader that I was thankful when we arrived on the Brooklyn side.

Of course the tens of thousands of spectators who perched and stood on every available space of the bridge and the banks of the river knew nothing of the danger. I alone, perhaps, was the only party in the transaction aware of it, and I was fortunate enough to keep Jumbo in good humor.

I may add that Jumbo was very much interested in what was going on around him. He knew just as well as myself that we were passing through an experiment (for had I not spent most of the previous night explaining to him what we were about to try and do), and as he looked down from the great promenade to the two lines of rails, one on each side, the two carriage drives, one on each side, and the railway underneath, all heavily freighted with human beings, he seemed to appreciate his high position. There were steamboats and ships sailing on the river, the beautiful islands lying out in the Bay, and the "City of Churches" in front of us, with all its array of spires, chimneys, and housetops. I can tell you, my readers, it was no ordinary event, and neither Jumbo nor I had much time or disposition to think of the great crowds of spectators who were so intently looking on. I may be pardoned if I say, for the information of my readers of both countries, that I know of nothing in the world equal to the sight which I took in at the moment I looked at the uplifted faces of that mighty crowd of the human family.

CHAPTER XII.

HOW JUMBO WAS IMPRESSED BY THE "GREAT BRIDGE"—VARIOUS INCIDENTS AND CONCLUSIONS.

Jumbo was very much amused at looking down into the river below. He did not evidently understand the meaning of a steamboat rushing along under his legs, so to speak, and I felt rather funny as I watched his keen, intelligent eye. Indeed, I may say, that when I and Jumbo are experimenting we always watch each other, "looking into each other's eyes, for the language of the heart," and so far we have been able to understand each other. So much so, that if Jumbo was not fast by the foot to a cable-chain of enormous strength, he would at a look from my eye into his follow me where-ever I might choose to lead him, and there is no power on earth, I think, that could prevent him obeying that look of command. But as I was saying Jumbo was constantly looking down below. He thought more about looking down to see what he was walking on than he did of looking up to the heavens, or at the gaping wondering crowd that occupied and lined the windows and house-tops, and which was to be seen on every available spot which commanded an elevated view.

As we looked down the funnels of the steamboats, and took a glance at the ships from a balloon-point of view, it was awfully interesting for me to answer Jumbo's questions, for my reader must remember that Jumbo had never seen a steamboat on the river. Indeed, if Jumbo had not been interested asking me questions about railways, and road ways, and steam cars, and steamboats, and about how it was that instead of walking down the streets lined with thousands upon thousands of people, we were walking on a set of planks suspended by wire spans at an elevation level with the tops of houses and warehouses, ten stories high I am sure, as I said, if it had not been for his many silent questions, spoken of above, I could never have got him over Brooklyn Bridge. It was the first bridge of the kind that he ever walked on, and I for one was very thankful when the journey was ended and we were once more on *terra firma.*

The sea of human faces that greeted us as we left the bridge to promenade the Brooklyn streets and avenues was a sight never to be forgotten.

An accident occurred after we left the bridge, on the Brooklyn side, as we passed along Fulton Street. The crowd was so vast and so anxious to see Jumbo, the "wonder of the world," that the people on the house-tops, on the balconies, and in the garret windows had to strain every nerve to look over each other, in order to get a sight of Jumbo. As we went up the street—one of Brooklyn's widest and finest business streets — the excitement became so intense and demonstrative, that it was a relief when we got through. The accident occurred to a little girl, eagerly stretched out of a four-story window to obtain a peep at Jumbo. She over-reached herself and fell to the ground, where she lost her young life. I only heard of this very sad accident a long time after it occurred, and at that distant time it caused me pain, as I thought of the poor mother's feelings when she raised up the shattered remains of her darling child.

It now comes to the time of ending this book about Jumbo and his keeper, your humble servant. It is my first and perhaps last attempt to give to the world our histories. It is my sincere hope that my humble efforts may be received as kindly by you as the writer has always been. If so, it is needless to say I shall be more than rewarded; and if poor, dear old Jumbo could but speak he would join in what I say.

FINIS.

Epilogue

Scott's account of his friend Jumbo ends before the great elephant's accidental death in Ontario only months after his book was published. Much of that tragedy has been chronicled elsewhere but it is fitting to include Scott's own account of the incident here, excerpted from the December 24th 1885 edition of the *Thomas County Cat.*:

> "I do not like to review the details of Jumbo's sudden death. He showed his affection for me to the last moment, and it seems that he realized the danger to which I was exposed. He first took care, as he saw the fatal train coming, that I should be saved, and quickly put me out of harm's way. Then he as quickly rolled Tom Thumb away from the track, and in so doing lost so much time that the engine

was upon him before he could move away. He was a king, and he faced death like a king."

The four newspaper articles that follow describe some of Scott's last years. Without Jumbo, his life had lost meaning. Forgotten and without friends, he died infirmed and alone in a poorhouse.

JUMBO'S OLD CHUM.

He Won't Return to England Because Jumbo's Carcass is Here.

Animal trainers are a queer lot as a rule, and show managers have to put up with many vagaries from them. They formed strong attachments for their big and sometimes ungainly pets, attachments one would hardly expect to exist tween a human being and wild beast.

A Case in point recently came under the notice of Mr. James L Hutchinson of the Barnum show, which serves well to illustrate what seems to be one of the chief traits in animals' character. When the Barnum people bought Jumbo in England they brought over to this country with him Matthew Scott, who for some 20 years had been the trainer and keeper of the huge, homely, but good-natured beast. Scott was Jumbo's guardian and constant companion during the pachyderm's brief but brilliant career in this country. When Jumbo met his death as the result of too much monkeying with a railroad train up in Canada, Scott was "all broke up," to use the vernacular. He was a restless, dissatisfied, pretty-well broken-up individual while the skin of his elephantine bedfellow was being stuffed and his skeleton cleaned and mounted for exhibition purposes. When the remains of Jumbo were added to the Barnum aggregation, Scott was put on exhibition with them. He seemed to have recovered some of his happiness then, and never tired of telling of the peaceful disposition, the kindly nature, and the altogether commendable habits is late chum.

When the Barnum show closed its season last October, Mr. Hutchinson told Scott that he would have no further use for him, and advised him to go back to England and accept the position at the

London zoological garden that was waiting for him. Scott said he would do so. On October 23 in Lynchburgh Virginia, Mr. Hutchinson paid Scott nearly $2000 which had accumulated in his hands as the old trainer's wages. Scott also received money to pay his passage back to Europe, in accordance with this agreement with the Barnum people. He bade everyone goodbye, left the show, and started for the city in time to take the steamer he had selected for Liverpool. That was the last seen or heard of him by the proprietors of the Barnum show until last week.

Mr. Hutchinson went up to the Bridgeport winter quarters then to see how things were progressing for the removal of the show's truck to this city. He was astonished shortly after leaving the city to meet Scott.

"Halloa, Scott, what are you doing here? Thought you were in England with your friends."

Scott stumbled in his words considerably and explained that he had made lots of friends in this country, rather liked it and thought he'd stay here for a while for rest as he had a good pile of money. He appeared to be a trifle ashamed of something, as if caught in a disreputable sort of proceeding. Mr. Hutchinson left him and went to the big barns and sheds of the company. But he could not forget Scott.

"Seen anything of Jumbo Scott around here lately?" he inquired casually of the people in the office. No, they hadn't. He determined to pursue his inquiries further, and solve the mystery of this man Scott's being in Bridgeport. So he went down to the elephant house. Yes, they had seen Scott; seen him frequently; almost daily in fact. Mr. Hutchinson followed the clue quietly and successfully and then it turned out that nearly every day since the show had been in winter quarters Scott had prowled about the barn chatted with the elephant men, and invariably wound up his call to the spot where the stuff Jumbo and his chained skeleton are stored. After a short, and so far as is known, silent communication with his dead friend, Scott would leave the place satisfied and go to his humble lodgings and Bridgeport. If the deceased Jumbo travels this season Scotty will want to, even if he isn't on the salary list.

— March 10, 1887 Wood County (Wisc.) Reporter

MAN WHO KEPT JUMBO DIES AT LAKEVIEW HOME

Matthew Scott, Veteran Animal Trainer, Had Disappeared From Public Life

NEVER RECOVERED FROM LOSS OF PET

Accompanied Pachyderm From London Zoo When Barnum Bought Animal

In the little holiday-bedecked chapel at Lakeview with only others of life's unfortunates, with whom he had been associated for the past two years, as mourners, simple services were said at 1:30 o'clock this afternoon over the body of

Matthew Scott, in former days one of the most expert of elephant trainers, personal guardian of the famous Jumbo and lifelong circus man. Rev. P. E. Mathias, pastor of the Kings Highway chapel, officiated. Following the service with six of his former associates acting as bearers the simple casket was carried to the little cemetery at the institution. Under lowering skies, far from his beloved England, the body of one of the most famous of animal trainers was laid to rest.

In his day "Scotty," as he was known not only to circus men but throughout the civilized world, was one of the most valued employees of the old Barnum & Bailey Circus. He was special keeper for the gigantic Jumbo in the old London zoo and refused to allow his charge to come to America alone when P. T. Barnum bought the famous elephant. In fact he had to be taken along, too, as Jumbo refused to mind other keepers. "Scotty" is claimed by circus men to have been the only human able to manage the elephant and the only one that Jumbo would mind without punishment.

During the years that Jumbo was a leading attraction in parades and performances in cities throughout the civilized world no one was allowed to attend to him but "Scotty." The animal and its keeper were attached to each other in a manner seldom seen in such cases. When Jumbo went to his tragic death in Canada "Scotty" was broken-hearted. It is said that he never had anything more to do with the elephant department and refused to touch them. On account of his expertness with animals he was retained in the small animal branch until he became a feeble, prematurely old man and was let go about six years ago.

It is a tradition among the older circus men that at midnight he always sat as if in a trance and responded to inquiries by saying that he was communing with the spirit of his beloved Jumbo. During the past five or six years he had been lost track of. His falling on evil ways are believed to have resulted from his never recovering grief occasioned by the death of his big friend of the elephant herd. Few of the old circus men knew that he was in Lakeview. Still fewer knew of his death.

Two years ago this month he was admitted to the institution broken down and suffering from kidney trouble. He suffered with this disease until his death and often was confined to his bed for days at a time. When able to be about, he acted as a sort of orderly. He seemed to be forgotten and wanted to be. No one of his old friends and circus companions called to see him during the two years. He frequently said that he had no home, no relatives and no one cared about him. Naturally uncommunicative about his past, he refused to tell anything about his past life. Few of those associating with him knew that he had been with the circus. It was not until last night that Lakeview officials learned of the former status of the little bent form. Accidentally it became known that the dead was once one of the big figures in the Circus world, had been honored by royalty and received the homage of thousands. He was 74 years old.

— December 24, 1914 Bridgeport Evening Farmer

CIRCUSMEN SAVE COMRADE FROM POTTER'S FIELD

Following the announcement of arrangements to bury Matthew Scott, Jumbo's former trainer, in the poor farm graves at Lakeview Home, circus men in the city and elsewhere came forward with a protest and under the direction of Al. Goulden, William O'Hara and Harry Mooney, the present Barnum & Bailey elephant trainer, arrangements for services have been made.

The funeral will be held on Monday at 2 o'clock. The body has been removed to the undertaking parlors of Cullinan & Mullins where it will be on view from 7 o'clock tonight. About 30 will follow the body to its last resting place next Monday.

— December 26, 1914 Bridgeport Evening Farmer

VETERAN CIRCUSMEN AT OBSEQUIES OF TRAINER OF "JUMBO"

Nearly 50 old time employees of the Barnum & Bailey Circus gathered about the remains of Matthew Scott yesterday to follow the body to its last resting place among circus men in the Park Cemetery. Services were held at 2:30 in the undertaking parlors of Cullinan and Mullins, where Rev. E. H. Kenyon, of St. Paul's Episcopal Church, read the burial ritual.

Following the service a large number of the old friends of "Scotty," as he was familiarly known from the time he brought Jumbo to America, followed the casket to the grave which was opened in the last remaining plot belonging to "The Tigers," a defunct organization composed of circus men. The pallbearers were William O'Hara, George Veay, Harry Mooney and Al. Goulden.

Among those who gathered about the bier were many who had traveled miles to pay respect to the departed, and who in former days had been closely associated with him.

— December 29, 1914 Bridgeport Evening Farmer

Manufactured by Amazon.ca
Bolton, ON